EXPLORERS WANTED!
At the North Pole
Simon Chapman

Also by Simon Chapman

In the Desert
In the Himalayas
In the Jungle
On Safari
Under the Sea
On the South Sea Islands
In the Wilderness

'Thrill-a-line style . . .
combining fascinating fact
with sound advice'
Books for Keeps

Simon Chapman
EXPLORERS
WANTED!

At the North Pole

EGMONT

EGMONT

We bring stories to life

For Phil Jumeau, polar explorer, for his help

First published in Great Britain in 2004
by Egmont Books Limited
239 Kensington High Street
London W8 6SA

Text and illustrations copyright © 2004 Simon Chapman

The moral rights of the author have been asserted

ISBN 1 4052 0731 0

1 3 5 7 9 10 8 6 4 2

A CIP catalogue record for this title
is available from the British Library

Printed and bound in Great Britain
by the CPI Group

CONTENTS

GREENLAND

3910 Qaanaaq

3970 Dundas

3984 Danmarkshavn

3962 Upernavik

3985 Cecilia's Pynt
3980 Ittoqqortoormiit

3963 Niaqornaliit

3961 Uummannaq

3953 Qeqertarsuaq

3952 Ilulissat

3951 Qasigiannguit

3950 Aasiaat

3910 Kangerlussuaq

Gaasiitsup Killeqarfia

Polarcirkel   Polarcirkel   Arctic Circle

3911 Sisimiut

3913 Ammassalik

3812 Maniitsoq

3900 NUUK   3805 Nuussuaq

KALAALLIT NUNAAT
GRØNLAND

SO ... YOU WANT TO EXPLORE THE NORTH POLE?

You want to ...

.. Drive a pack of huskies across the **frozen Arctic** wastes ...?

Fend off **polar bears** and packs of **ravenous Arctic foxes** ...?

Sledge through the land of the midnight sun ...?
If the answer is **YES**, then this is the book for you.

Read on to get wise to the essentials of how to survive in this freezing land of snow and ice, how to cross the perilous ice floes and how to navigate where the only direction you can go is south! Find out about the explorers who tried before you; some who succeeded and some who didn't make it, in this freezer at the top of the world.

Mission Dossier

Your mission is to find the lost 'Airship *Italia*'.

Timeline:

May 23rd 1928.
Italian aviator General Umberto Nobile sets off northwards in an airship from the Arctic island of Svalbard, his aim to cross the pole and investigate rumours that there are undiscovered land masses among the shifting ice floes.

May 25th 1928.
A distress signal was received:

'Too much weight of ice encrusting "envelope" ... forced down ...'

Radio contact was lost. An international rescue mission was set in motion. Seaplanes scoured the Arctic Ocean. Ice-breaking ships smashed their way through the pack ice and eventually Nobile and most of his crew were found (you can read what happened in Chapter 8). But neither the airship, nor the six unfortunate Italians who were still on it when it blew away in the wind after it had crashed were ever discovered. What happened to them, nobody knows. Until now, that is …

January: A satellite image has shown up a long, dark shape on the ice, uncovered in the pack ice close to Murrelet Island, north of Greenland. Could this be the *Italia*? Your task is to go there and find out.

Warning: You have to act fast. By the time you get your expedition together it is late March. Soon the warming spring temperatures will be thawing the polar ice sheet, breaking it up. Then the ice carrying the airship – if that's what it is – will float off. You will have lost your chance to find it, possibly forever.

Where are you going?

The Arctic. The top of the world. It's extremely cold, bare and windswept and for the most part covered with snow and ice. Around the edges there is land like the huge mountainous islands of Greenland and Svalbard, but over the pole itself there is just ice. Frozen water, the ice cap's shape is constantly changing as its edges melt in the

SUMMER
IN THE
ARCTIC
CIRCLE

summer and refreeze in the winter. Meanwhile, ocean currents ram the ice sheets together, endlessly splitting them apart and rejoining them in different ways. Virtually nothing grows here and all life looks to the sea for food.

Further south, on the lands fringing the Arctic Circle is the tundra, a wilderness of knee-high forests and mossy bog land, teeming with life for two or three short months in the summer, frozen solid for the rest of the year.

The seasons are extreme. In the height of Northern summer there is continual daylight. With the tilt of the Earth on its axis, at this time of year, the northern part is always pointed towards the sun. On the ground, you see the sun dip but never go below the horizon. This is the time when the ice floes break up, the snow on the tundra melts and birds like swans and geese migrate north to feed, before the days become shorter and the cold comes again. By Northern midwinter, the Arctic is smothered by continual darkness. Temperatures plummet and most of the animals and birds (that are able to) move south to survive.

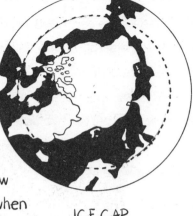

ICE CAP
SUMMER

ICE CAP WINTER

Of course at the other end of the planet, the Antarctic, the same climatic switch happens but the other way around. Winter in the Arctic is summer in the Antarctic. While the

north has continual night, the south has continual day –
and vice versa in the Antarctic summer/Arctic winter.

But what other differences exist between life at the two
Poles? For a start, the Antarctic has a solid continental
land mass underneath it. There are even desert valleys
where no snow ever falls. But for the most part, covered
with snow and ice, the two polar areas look the same. Many
of the animals living at the ends of the Earth are similar.
Some are the same, but there are differences.

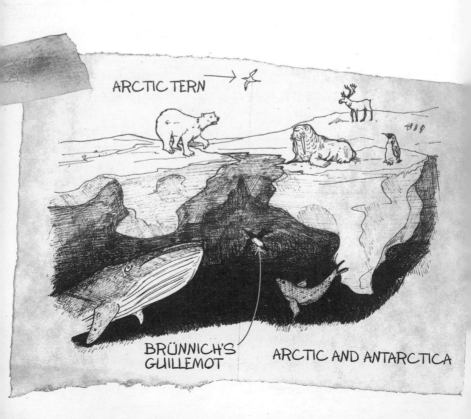

ARCTIC TERN →

BRÜNNICH'S
GUILLEMOT

ARCTIC AND ANTARCTICA

Look at this picture. Choose whether the creatures live in the **north**, **south** or **both**.

1. Polar bear
2. Seal
3. Walrus
4. Minke whale
5. Caribou
6. Emperor penguin
7. Brünnich's Guillemot
8. Arctic tern

Answers on pages 9–10

So, what's it actually like in the Arctic?

Before you set off, you're going to need to know what the conditions are like ...

Pack Ice. A flat expanse of dazzling white as far as you can see in all directions. The sun is low in the sky casting your shadow out across the whiteness. A strong wind blows across you, the tiny crystals of ice it carries with it sting any exposed skin in the crisp coldness. Wrapped up in your down-filled coat and snow boots you feel warm enough but in the back of your mind you know it wouldn't take much to tip the balance and turn this into a survival situation, one where you wouldn't stand much chance of coming out alive.

A change in the weather could have you stumbling through total whiteout. Almost instantly you could become disorientated - lost!

Lose a glove and the minus 14 degrees °C temperature (knocked down to a chilly minus 34 °C by that wind) would soon give your fingers frostbite. They would go numb and eventually freeze hard. They might even break off!

WHITEOUT!

Fall through a patch of thin ice and your end could come even quicker. If the cold shock didn't give you a heart attack, and you managed to get back on to the surface, you would have to get warmed up within minutes before the extreme cold sapped your strength, your mind clouded and you lost consciousness …

And what if you met a **polar bear**? The Earth's largest land predator would make easy meat out of you...

If you thought surviving here was going to be easy, then think again. You've not only got to survive but you've got to cross this white wilderness. It's obvious you'll need training and all the right gear if you're to stand any chance at all.

ANSWERS from page 7

1. **North.**
2. **Both** – Though the types at either Pole are different.
3. **North.**
4. **Both** – Some types of whale migrate to feed in the plankton-rich waters at both ends of the Earth.
5. **North.** Antarctica is cut off from the other continents by hundreds of kilometres of sea. Land animals never got there.

6. **South.** Note: Some types of penguin live in warmer waters, like around Australia and New Zealand, but never in the Northern Hemisphere. All of those Christmas cards with penguins talking to polar bears are wrong. They would never meet nor even know of each others' existence!

7. **North.** Notice that it looks just like a penguin. Auks (guillemots included) live similar fish-hunting lives to penguins, but they can fly. They often live in huge cliff-edge colonies out of reach of predators like Arctic foxes.

8. **Both.** Amazingly, Arctic terns can be seen close to both poles. They have the longest migration route of any bird.

Your score

0-3: Lousy. Make your mind up which Pole you are trying to get to before you set off exploring.

4-6: Middling but acceptable at this early stage in the expedition.

7-8: Excellent. An Arctic explorer in the making! You're fully 'sussed' already.

Chapter 1
DRESSING WARM, EATING WARM

Surviving the extreme cold; that's your primary consideration. Before you start kitting yourself out for your expedition to look for Nobile's lost airship, you first ought to know what the cold can do to you.

Prolonged cold (not necessarily below freezing point) combined with exhaustion and lack of food leads to …

Hypothermia. Your body is losing heat faster than it can generate it. You feel overwhelmingly tired (though you may have sudden bursts of energy). You lose coordination and stumble more often. Your vision may blur. You may have headaches or behave strangely. You need warming up before you lose consciousness. Get out of the wind. Replace wet clothes with dry ones. Huddle up with someone warm. Exposure can kill.

There is also 'immersion hypothermia'. This is when you suddenly become chilled by falling into freezing cold water. Water conducts heat away from your body twenty-five times as quickly as air. You have to put on dry clothing. You have to warm up fast.

Frostbite. Freezing temperatures can freeze your skin and body parts, most often fingers and toes. In extreme cases, whole feet can freeze solid. This happened to Robert Peary, the first person to get to the North Pole (he claimed ... more about this in Chapter 6). On his second (unsuccessful) attempt in 1905, both his feet froze solid. The flesh was white up to beyond his ankles.

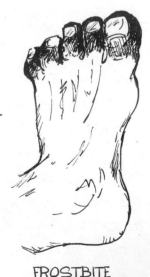

FROSTBITE

Still, he carried on, knowing that the pain would be too intense if his feet were warmed up. When Matt Henson, his assistant, eventually cut off Peary's boots, several toes iced on to the leather came off too. When Peary did eventually get to the Pole in 1909 (or did he?), it was with only one little toe on each foot.

Don't let this happen to you. Watch out for the prickly sensation as your skin starts to freeze (**frost nip**) or the waxy sheen it develops as it starts to go numb. Pull silly faces to keep the blood flowing through your face (yes, really!). If one of your feet is affected, put it against a friend's stomach or in their armpit to gently warm it. Don't rub it with snow (a traditional remedy) or put it close to a fire to heat up. Both will make things worse – and much more painful.

If the freezing of your body tissue is deeper, your flesh will go hard, swollen and look red, pebbly and possibly blistered too. That frozen tissue is dead. If you thaw it now, it will be **extremely painful**. Gangrene may set in. The poisons in your blood will probably kill you if untreated. This is one reason why Peary carried on. If you have frostbite that advanced, don't cut off toes like explorers in the past did. These days it can be treated.

How can you stop this happening to you? This trip is not worth losing your toes for. You'll have to think how to 'dress warm' and how you can 'eat warm' – that is take food with you that is absolutely stacked with energy.

First of all, get kitted out. If you think like an Inuit, you won't go far wrong. After all, these Arctic people have been living up here, in what to you appears an empty freezing whiteness, for thousands of years.

This is the clothing and kit you'll be wearing. Compare it with what an Inuit might wear. Their traditional clothing, made of sealskin or reindeer hide is often just as good, sometimes even better than modern 'high-tech' gear.

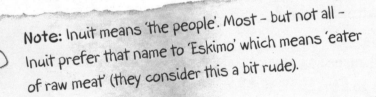

Note: Inuit means 'the people'. Most – but not all – Inuit prefer that name to 'Eskimo' which means 'eater of raw meat' (they consider this a bit rude).

FLEECE

OUTER MITTENS
& INNER GLOVES

SNOW
GOGGLES/
SUNGLASSES

BALACLAVA

SNOW
BOOTS

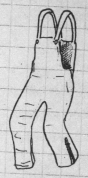

THERMAL
UNDERWEAR

SALOPETTES

- Outer coat and salopettes (you could wear an all-in-one body suit but this makes going to the toilet difficult).
- Fleece pullover.
- Thermal underwear/tracksuit trousers.
- Snow boots with thermal inners.
- Mittens with thermal inners (note the clips so you don't lose them).
- Balaclava hat.
- Snow goggles/sunglasses.

Inuit kit

- Fur-lined mukluk boots.
- Caribou (reindeer) fur coat. Often this has the fur on the inside as the trapped air provides good insulation to stop body heat conducting out. There is Arctic fox fur round the hood and cuffs. The skin on the outside is windproof, though not totally waterproof (that would trap any sweat inside). For kayaking on the sea, waterproof 'kagoules' made out of seal guts were often worn.
- Mittens.
- Snow goggles made of seal hide with eye slits cut across them. You could improvise similar goggles if you lost yours. Smearing black charcoal under your eyes also helps reduce glare.

You don't want to get snow blindness where your eyes are too painful to open and you stream tears.

INUIT

SEAL-HIDE
GOGGLES

Now, let's look at that coat you're wearing in more detail. It is made of special 'breathable' fabric that is windproof and waterproof from the outside but allows water vapour to escape from inside, but the basic idea is the same as the Inuit parka. Can you work out what some of the features are there for?

Match the design feature with its purpose ...

Design Feature	What it does
1. Inner elasticated 'skirt'	A. Water vapour from your breath will freeze here rather than on your face.
2. Fur 'trim'	B. Stops warm air bellowing out when you lift your arms.
3. Snug-fitting inner cuffs	C. Lets in cold air to cool you down.
4. Side zips	D. Stops snow blowing up.

Answers on page 20

Surprisingly, you may find that one of your biggest problems is keeping cool. If you are exerting yourself cross-country skiing or even building an igloo, you'll find yourself getting uncomfortably hot under all that insulating clobber. (This is incidentally a big problem for polar bears - find out what they do about it in Chapter 5.)

Here is some other stuff you'll be taking with you.

- **Spare clothes.** Two complete sets of, in waterproof bags.
- **Trainers.** To wear around camp.
- **Suncream.** The sun's rays may not be as strong as further south but there's all that snow to reflect off. Your face - and especially your nose and lips will become seriously burnt - skin peeling and painful - unless you apply lots of sunblock.
- **GPS** (satellite Global Positioning System)
- **Compass**
- **Cross-country skis.** These have special 'skins' fixed on the bottoms so they can slide forwards but not back. The bindings attach to the front of your boots so you can lift the heel up but not the toe which stays fixed to the ski as you slide along.

ICE-AXE

SLEEP MAT

FLARE GUN
AND FLARES

STOVE

JACKET

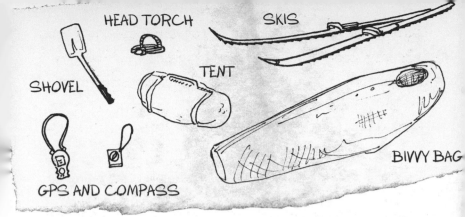

HEAD TORCH
SKIS
TENT
SHOVEL
BIVVY BAG
GPS AND COMPASS

- Ski poles
- Ice-axe
- Ropes
- Flare gun
- Torch
- Tent
- Sleeping bag

- Bivvy bag. Waterproof, breathable outer cover for sleeping bag, useful if you have to sleep out in the open.
- Inflatable sleep mat
- Snow shovel
- Stove and fuel

Kit Quiz

Look at this kit list. What could you use to:

1. Signal for help or scare off a polar bear?
2. Clear away ice blocking the path of your sledge?
3. Wear after you fell through thin ice?
4. Probe the ice ahead to check if it is thick enough to walk on?
5. Find out exactly where you are?
6. Melt ice to provide drinking water?
7. Insulate you from the cold ice beneath your tent?
8. Move faster than just walking?

Answers on page 23

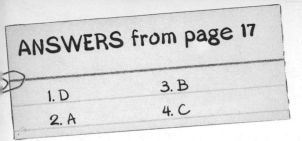
The amount of stuff you are taking certainly is mounting up and we haven't even sorted out your food yet. For that you have to think about what you can eat that has maximum energy and minimum weight. It helps to be prepared ... otherwise you might find yourself in similar circumstances to earlier Arctic explorers who ended up eating ...

· **Guillemots** (penguin-like sea birds). In 1829, Royal Navy captain John Ross's paddle steamer became stuck in the ice for four years. His crew must have eaten hundreds of these oily birds. Usually raw.

· **Polar bears** - Though eating polar bear livers can kill you as they contain potentially lethal doses of Vitamin A.

· Leathery **lichen** scraped from rocks.

· Ground-up **caribou bones** dug out of the frozen ground.

· Their own boots. Shoe **leather** has some food value but it has to be boiled for a long, long time before it's soft enough to eat.

· Each other. Captain John Franklin, lost in the Arctic tundra in 1822, suspected some members of his crew of **cannibalism** when others did not return from their scouting mission.

Leather boots? Cannibalism? Let's sort you out before you start to find that sort of thing tempting. Take a look at this sensibly.

A grown man needs to intake around **12,000** kilojoules (kJ) of energy daily.

Add another **6,000** for working strenuously

and another **6,000** to cope with the cold; that adds up to a

whopping **24,000** kilojoules of food energy for an Arctic explorer. Each day.

'Eating Warm': Food Provisions Quiz

Here are the energy values of **100 grams** of some types of food you could take.

Food	Energy stored in 100 grams	Notes
Lard	3,600 kJ	Pure animal fat.
Pemmican	3,100 kJ	a mixture of dried meat, animal fat, fruit, nuts and grains.
Mixed Nuts	2,800 kJ	Macadamia nuts are particularly high in stored energy.

Food	Energy stored in 100 grams	Notes
Chocolate	2,400 kJ	
Muesli	1,700 kJ	A mixture of nuts and grains. Also contains fibre, which helps you digest your food.
Cheese	1,400 kJ	Contains calcium and protein (like meat).
Pasta	1,200 kJ	
Bread	900 kJ	Bulky.
Rice	500 kJ	
Fresh fruit	50-100 kJ	Bulky.

1. Choose three foods you would take.
2. Which three foods would there be little point in taking?
3. Which food would give you energy but would be disgusting to eat?
4. Which food would be good to take for its morale-boosting effect?
5. Which food gives you a good balance of different food types?

Answers on pages 24-25

ANSWERS from page 19

1. flare gun
2. ice-axe
3. spare clothes
4. ski poles or ice-axe

5. GPS
6. stove and fuel
7. inflatable sleep mat
8. cross-country skis.

Clothes sorted. Equipment sorted. Food sorted. Ready to go? Look how much stuff you'll be taking.; how are you going to carry all of that? Of course it would be rather nice to have the use of a 'Sno-cat' expedition vehicle as used to cross the Antarctic land mass in 1955-58. But there's the problem. **Land mass.** This is the North Pole we're dealing with, not the South. At some point you'll be travelling across sea ice and quite simply any large motor vehicle would crack it and sink through ... although this wouldn't be a problem if you had a vehicle like Snowbird which was used on an attempt to cross the ice-bound Bering Strait between Siberia and Alaska in 2003. Snowbird has caterpillar tracks and gigantic floating screws on each side to pull itself through floating ice. It hasn't succeeded ...yet.

How about something smaller? Skidoos - snowmobiles are fast and look awfully good fun to zoom around on. Unfortunately none was available at the start point of your trip, at the Inuit coastal settlement of Ninnuvulik. So it's back to more traditional methods of transport - sledge and dog power. You've arranged for a driver, Jimmy Asecaq, and a pack of husky dogs to meet you at Ninnuvulik. Jimmy will train you how to handle the dogs and sledge, then together you will set out across the pack ice in search of Nobile's lost airship.

But first you've got to get to Ninnuvulik. You've got to cross the boggy tundra.

ANSWERS from pages 21-22

Keep track of your score . . .

1. Pemmican, mixed nuts	3 points each
Muesli, chocolate, cheese, pasta	2 points each
Bread, rice	1 point each
Fruit	0 points

2. **Fresh fruit** is too bulky and heavy. **Rice**, though filling, gives you less energy than pasta. **Bread** is bulky for the energy it provides you with. (1 point each)

3. **Lard**. The Inuit eat pure seal blubber for energy, though. You could always mix lard with nuts and chocolate to make it more palatable. (1 point)

4. Chocolate! Notice 10 portions of 100 grams, 10 x **2,400** = **24,000** kilojoules. That means 1 kilogram of chocolate will give you your daily energy intake. No. You can't JUST take that! You have to have a balanced diet. (1 point)

5. Pemmican (2 points) or mixed nuts (1 point); both are staple choices on Arctic expeditions.

Your score (out of 16)

15–16. Rename yourself 'Fridtjof Nansen' and off you go! You're a born polar explorer!

12–14. You'll be fine. Enjoy eating all that monotonous pemmican on your gruelling Arctic slog.

11 and below. This is serious. If you can't even get your food organised then you should quit the expedition while you are still alive.

Chapter 2
ACROSS THE TUNDRA

Direction North: Altitude 1,000 metres, Speed 330 kph.
It's clear, looking down, that winter is ending. There are
patches where the snow has started to melt on the tundra.
Caribou are congregating in large herds and moving to
where the grazing is good. You can see hundreds of them.
The lines of marching animals spread into the distance. Like
explorers who came here one and two hundred years ago,
you could be fooled into believing that this was a land of
plenty. With so much meat on the hoof there must be lush
plant life to feed on. What you can see in your plane that they
couldn't down on the ground is that these are the only
caribou for hundreds of kilometres. The rest of the tundra is
virtually empty of large wildlife. The caribou you can see now
have eaten all the available food and are migrating to where
the moss and the lichen grow thicker. It could be many years
before they return to this area and the moss and lichen have
grown back after all that nibbling. All the plants that grow
here are really slow-growing. Much of the year it is simply

too cold, too dark or they are covered with snow. There is only a month or two of proper growing time in each year. Those low bushes could be hundreds of years old.

What does it take to be a plant of the tundra? Life is tough out here. You have to be tough to survive.

Trials of the Tundra: Quiz

Match the condition with how the plants cope with it.

Conditions	What the plant does about it
1. Frequent storm-force winds	A. Shallow roots
2. Ground permanently frozen not far below surface	B. Special antifreeze chemicals in cells stop water in the cells freezing and expanding, which would burst the cells.
3. Ground waterlogged when not frozen.	C. Thrives when totally soaking.
4. Freezing conditions	D. Shuts down for most of year.
5. Darkness for long periods	E. Ground-hugging

Answers on page 34

Which kind of plants can put up with this degree of punishment?

Mosses - They like life soggy.

Lichens - A combination of plant and fungus. Lichens can live on bare rock! Some lichens like 'rock tripe' make a particularly unappetising survival food if boiled up into an acid-tasting slime. Expeditions of explorers lost in the tundra, like John Franklin's in 1822, have been known to live on this for months on end … though they did become so weak their hands shook too much to fire their rifles straight when they finally did come across some tasty-looking caribou.

CLUB MOSS

LICHEN

Flat trees - The Arctic willow is impossible to blow over as it grows level to the ground. The further south you go and in sheltered valleys, the conditions become slightly easier. You find more trees struggling to grow up until eventually the tundra turns into the 'taiga' forest.

ARCTIC WILLOW

The tundra is a fragile place. Nature here recovers so slowly from any damage that people have to tread carefully – literally. It takes years for plants to re-colonise a line of muddy footprints. The tracks from vehicles like tractors and cranes used to assemble the pipelines that carry the oil and gas found in the Siberian and Alaskan tundra show up as twin black scar lines against the green vegetation. Underneath, only a metre down, the ground is frozen solid with permafrost. This only slightly melts in

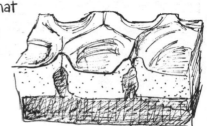

FORMATION OF A
TUNDRA POLYGON

the height of the summer. Any meltwater from the winter snows simply sits on top of it. Then the whole tundra becomes a soggy mass of spongy ground and little lakes.

Eco Alert!

The fact that much of the permafrost appears to be melting is worrying. Normally ice-firm land has subsided, damaging houses and roads. Winters haven't been as cold in recent years and sometimes the geese and swans don't even bother to migrate away. Are these signs of global warming?

In some places you see piles of stones at regular intervals as though someone's put them there. They sit along the edges of what looks from the air like regular pentagon and hexagon shapes. They're totally natural. It's that winter freeze and summer thaw that's moved the rocks and made these 'tundra polygons'. Here's how ...

Water expands (gets bigger) when it freezes. When the sodden ground freezes in winter the expanding ice creates a slight dome, which starts growing outwards, moving pebbles and stones with it. Where the stones pushed outwards from different centres meet, ridges (the edges of the polygons) are formed.

Another freezing effect is the formation of 'pingos'. These are conical hills, up to a hundred metres high. They look like mini-volcanoes but are formed by underground freezing and

thawing, concentrating the water and forcing up a pyramid of ice. All of this makes the tundra a terrain which is very difficult to cross, certainly if you are laden down with equipment to mount a polar expedition. That's why you decided to fly this section of your journey. Just surviving down there is hard, but many animals do. Some even stick it out throughout the whole year like *caribou, musk oxen, lemmings, wolves, Arctic foxes, snowy owls.*

Animal Quiz

First, here's some information.

A. **Musk ox.** They line up with hooked horns facing outwards. Sometimes they charge. With bulls weighing in at around 400 kg, that is a scary proposition – it's not as though there are any trees you can climb or hide behind.

MUSK OXEN

B. **Wolf.** Many tundra wolves are white.

WHITE WOLF

C. **Lemming.** These rodents breed so successfully in warmer years that they get stressed out with each other trying to find food and decent places to live. Often, they all

LEMMING

swarm off together - into rivers and sometimes (accidentally) over cliffs. A famous nature film around fifty years ago showed hundreds tumbling over a cliff, but it has since turned out that the camera crew was chasing them. The lemmings weren't suicidal, they were just scared.

D. **Arctic fox.** These don't hibernate and in the long, dark winters will go for just about anything - lemmings, ground-dwelling birds, dead caribou, and sick explorers ... In 1741, the naturalist Wilhelm Stellar was shipwrecked on a

ARCTIC FOX

Siberian island along with forty-four of his crew, many of whom were injured or sick. The healthy men used timbers from their ship to make shelter against the gales and driving rain which lashed the island but soon had another problem to contend with, hordes of marauding 'blue' foxes. Nipping at dead and injured men and biting bits off them was far easier for the foxes than chasing the island's birds to eat. One poor man got bitten in rather an embarrassing place and had quite a tug of war with one of the foxes. His mistake had been to go outside for a pee during the night!

Note: Most Arctic foxes only grow their thick white fur coat in winter. The rest of the time they are mottled grey.

E. Snowy Owl. All over white with soft
feathers that make no sound as they flap,
snowy owls are genuine
'stealth' attackers, virtually
impossibly to detect for any poor
lemming that sticks its head out of its
snow tunnel.

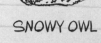

SNOWY OWL

F. Caribou. This is the name of the wild
deer in Alaska and Canada. Both
sexes have antlers. European ones,
especially the tame herds, used for
meat and milk by Arctic people like the
Lapps of Finland and Russia, are
called reindeer.

CARIBOU

Can you remember which of these animals . . .

1. . . . is know as a reindeer in Europe?
2. . . . used to be said to be suicidal as masses of them
   occasionally fall off cliffs together?
3. . . . is a 'stealth' killer (if you are a lemming)?
4. . . . forms into a circle for protection, heads facing outwards?
5. . . . is the major hunter of the tundra?
6. . . . is a scavenger that won't miss any opportunity for a meal?

Answers on page 34

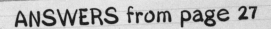

ANSWERS from page 27

1. E   2. A   3. C   4. B   5. D

ANSWERS from page 33

1. F – Caribou.   4. A – Musk Ox.
2. C – Lemming.   5. B – Wolf.
3. E – Snowy Owl.   6. D – Arctic Fox.

These animals are residents. They stay in the tundra the whole year round. There are many others though that just come up for the summer season.

· Brown bears
· Moose
· Whooper swans
· Snow geese

…And millions of midges and mosquitoes which somehow have managed to stay dormant all the way through the freezing winter and come out just as soon as it gets warmer as if just to stop everybody else having a good time. One particular nasty is the warble fly. It lays its eggs in the underside fur of

MOSQUITO

caribou. When they hatch, the maggots burrow under the deer's skin,

feasting on its living flesh until they drop off, pupate and turn into fully grown flies, ready to find some other poor caribou.

WARBLE FLY
AND MAGGOT

Fortunately for you, being plagued by clouds of biting insects is not going to be a problem. Where you are going will be far too cold and desolate for most of the denizens of the tundra to survive - or you if you aren't properly equipped. As your plane dips down towards a craggy coastline dotted with around ten widely spaced out buildings that must be the Inuit village of Ninnuvulik, it strikes you that the sea ahead of that coast is not grey or blue or even moving. It is pure, flat white.

NINNUVULIK

Chapter 3
DOG POWER

Dog power – that's how you're going to eat up the distances across the pack ice in your search for Nobile's lost airship. Although these days snowmobiles could be used as your transport, there are questions over high cost, carrying all the fuel you need and mechanical reliability. Dogs don't break down often and as the famous Norwegian explorer Roald Amundsen found in 1911 when he was the first man to reach the South Pole, if they do croak, you can always feed them to the others.

This is your team: Snowy, Gripper, Tallulah, Twinkle, Gnasher, Fang and Bonzo (actually this is what you call them, as you can't remember their Inuit names). These dogs are Greenlander huskies, tough working dogs, bred to pull sledges and survive the extreme cold. They will quite happily sleep in minus 30

degree blizzards, wrapping their bushy tails over their heads and ignoring the snow as it drifts round them.

They will exist on a diet of half-frozen seal or walrus meat. These dogs are seriously tough and you will have to be too, if you want to control them.

Over the next few days, your guide (and expert dog-handler) Jimmy Asecaq shows you how to handle your team. It's all about showing them that you are now the leader of their pack. They must learn to move out of the way when you pass and to understand and obey your commands. You must be the one to feed them – though don't go too close – don't hold your hand out and certainly don't stroke or pat them – these vicious canines could quite easily bite off a finger or two along with that tasty morsel of seal meat!

To pull the sledge effectively, each of the dogs has its special position in the team.

Snowy is the lead dog. He has to find and follow the trail, set the pace and listen to your commands. This is the most stressful position to be in, the first to meet any hazard from thin ice to polar bears. Once in a while you might want to swap him with one of the others.

Next come **Fang** and **Bonzo**. They are your 'swing' dogs that help you turn and also set the pace.

Then there are **Gripper** and **Gnasher**, big, strong dogs to provide power.

And at the back…
… **Tallulah** and **Twinkle**: they are the 'wheel' dogs that help you turn.

These are the commands, to which they respond … with Jimmy at least …

'Hike Up!'	Let's go
'Whoa!'	Stop
'Gee!'	Right
'Haw!'	Right
'Easy!'	Slow down

To stop your sledge, you've also got a u-shaped steel bar 'brake' that you can press and a studded rubber 'drag' mat to slow it. As a last resort, if they don't work with an overeager dog team, there are snow-hook anchors you can throw down.

What about 'Mush'? Isn't that what you should say to make your dogs go? The answer is **Yes** if you train them. It's thought that 'Mush' comes from Canada, where French speakers would say 'Marche', which means 'Walk'.

To be honest, until you convince your team that you're **Top Dog** none of these commands will have much effect. At the start all your dogs will do when you're in charge is just run and run. The only way to stop them is to throw down the snow hooks ...

Finally the day comes when Jimmy decides you're ready to set off across the pack ice. You will each drive a sledge so that there is some back-up if one of you should get into trouble. Otherwise, you will be on your own.

The weather has become colder over the last few days, which your guide says should give you a good clear run across the vast white flatness of frozen-over sea that lies ahead of you. Nevertheless, you will have to keep alert. In

that whiteness there are areas of thin ice or holes that you and your team could fall through into the sea. There are also pressure ridges where plates of pack ice have pushed into each other and squashed upwards or one has slid over the other. Though some pressure ridges are little more than wrinkles on the ice, others are metres high with tumbled blue blocks of sea ice. Here you need to look for ways past the obstacles. Occasionally you have to unhitch your dogs and manhandle your sledge and gear across the ice.

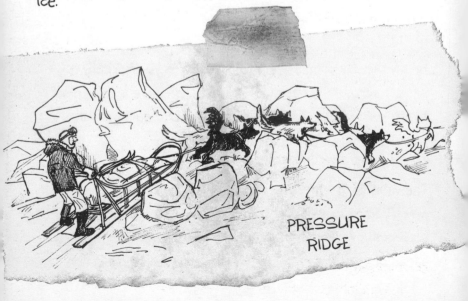

PRESSURE RIDGE

To begin with the sky is clear and you feel you are making good progress towards the bumps on the horizon, which you hope is Murrelet

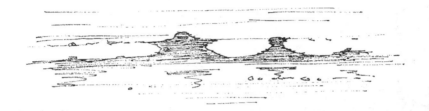

Island. But it's hard to tell. In such crisp clear air the distances are deceptive, as distant objects are as in-focus as near ones. Also layers of super-cold air can cause light rays to bend (refract). Ice, water and snow can reflect the light so some of the things you see may not be really there.

Arctic Illusions - Quiz

1. Only one of these optical illusions seen by Arctic travellers is made up. Which one?

   A. A range of mountains.

   B. A forest.

   C. An oasis with palm trees.

   D. Mid-air mountains.

   E. An upside-down sailing ship flying through the air.

2. A craggy mountain with two glaciers was spotted by a Swedish explorer. What was he really looking at?

3. After dark you see swirling greenish 'curtains' of light lighting up the night sky. What do you think causes them?

A. An optical illusion where the moonlight is distorted in the cold Arctic air.

B. You are seeing the lights from settlements ahead reflected in airborne ice crystals.

C. Charged particles from the sun, attracted by the Earth's magnetic field, hitting air molecules causing them to give off light.

Answers on pages 46-47

On the flat ice north of Ninnuvulik you have hours to think about illusions like this. The terrain is monotonous, continual flat whiteness and you have to stop your mind from wandering too much and keep an eye out for pressure ridges or areas of thin ice.

Your first camp feels so exposed. A stiff breeze has started to blow and the parts of your face exposed under the goggles feel wind-burnt. You heap up snow around the 'skirt' you've sewn on to your dome tent. The extra weight should hold the sides down and stop the wind catching under the light structure. In front of your tent, Jimmy advises you to dig a low trench with your snow shovel. For one thing it will let you sit comfortably while you use the stove to cook up your meal of packet soup, cheese and pasta. Secondly, the snow you remove can be melted for drinking water. You'll soon find that melting snow to get enough water to drink will become one of the chores of the trip. Snow is full of trapped air which, as with your clothing, prevents heat conducting through it. Melting snow wastes more of your precious fuel than melting ice. Unfortunately there is no freshwater ice to melt, only sea ice which could be difficult to get and would be salty in any case.

How to melt snow the Inuit way

1. Find a slight slope – a mound of snow will do.
2. Set up a block of snow above a burning lump of seal blubber and hollow out a small pool for the melted water to collect in.
3. The smoke from the burning blubber will have dirtied the water, so hollow out a series of pools, each beneath the other.
4. Cut a passage so that meltwater can flow from one pool to the next and put a lump of soft snow in each gap.
5. The soft snow will filter the dirty water. The more pools and filters you have, the cleaner the water at the bottom.

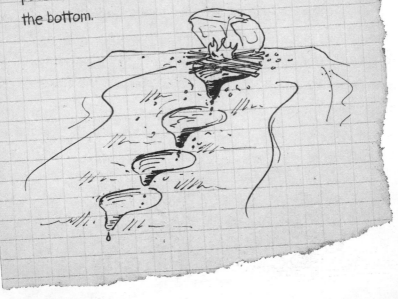

The night passes uneventfully. In fact you are surprised how warm it was with two of you in the tent. You hitch up the dogs and set off. Visibility is poorer today. It's hard to make out where the ice ends and the sky begins.

Hours pass.

Above the sound of the patter of the dogs' feet and noise of the sled runners on the ice you can make out a faint whine - like a chainsaw or maybe a motorbike. Something is approaching you. It's too distant to make out its shape but judging from the sound, you think it must be a snowmobile. As it draws nearer, you can make out the rider and something - or someone - else slumped across the back behind him. Whatever it is looks like
a body - but of what?

You shout 'Whoa!' at the dogs and when that doesn't slow them, press on the brake, then throw out the snow hooks to bring your team to a halt.

ANSWERS from pages 41–42

1. C. A desert mirage, but all the others have been seen on many occasions. The ship illusion is called the 'Flying Dutchman effect', named after a famous ghost ship that was said to sail the oceans. It's a type of mirage caused when a layer of cool air is trapped beneath a layer of warm air. The light rays curve but you see the ship – or a view of the sea, or some distant island – as if it were on a straight line, up in the sky. A bogus set of Mirage Mountains made Captain John Ross of the Royal Navy a laughing stock. Searching for the famed North-west Passage sea route through the arctic ice in 1822, he reported it to be impossible as there were mountains in the way. But the 'Croker' mountain range did not exist. Perhaps Ross had been looking at a mirage of a distant island. Ross returned in 1829 determined to restore his reputation. This time his ship became stuck in the ice. It took four years for he and his crew to escape.

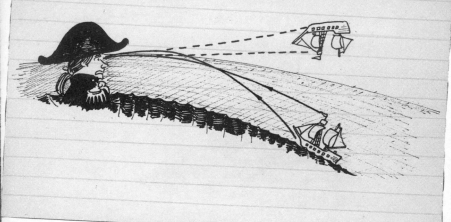

2. A walrus. I wonder what the Swede's reaction was when he found that he was actually really close to a two-tonne tusked beast!

3. C. What you are seeing is the **Aurora Borealis** or 'Northern Lights' caused when charged particles from the sun, channelled by the Earth's magnetic field, collide with oxygen and nitrogen atoms in the atmosphere, causing them to give off light. The aurora can come in a range of colours – most often yellowy green, sometimes violet, blue or red depending on which atoms are giving out the energy. Close to the South Pole there is a similar effect called the **Aurora Australis**.

Chapter 4
SHOOTING SEALS

It's a seal. Obviously dead. You can see a wound and bright-red blood dribbling down the animal's chest and dropping on to the snow as the snowmobile pulls up. Its rider is wrapped up against the chill – and armed. He has a rifle slung across his back.

As the man dismounts and approaches, your gaze is still fixed on the seal's blood staining the snow. This is the only animal you have seen in two days on the pack ice and it has been shot dead.

Killing the wildlife - how do you feel about this? You feel
a little shocked but, then again, the nearest shop is at
Ninnuvulik, 60 kilometres away. You've been there and you've
seen for yourself that there is not exactly a huge choice -
tins of meat and fish, dried pasta, blankets, batteries -
essentials only. Any other purchases are a plane or boatride
(in the high summer only when the pack ice has melted)
away. Out here in the high Arctic you have to survive on what
you can hunt or find. Many Inuit - like the man now standing
before you - are keen to continue their traditional lifestyles,
although with modern equipment: snowmobiles instead of
huskies and sledges, high-powered rifles replacing bone-
tipped harpoons. This man - Kuraluk (you recognise him
from Ninnuvulik) will put this dead harp seal to good use.
The skin will be used for clothing, with the sinews used for
thread. The flesh will be eaten. The blubber will be used as
fuel for heating and lighting.

Kuraluk says getting the seal was just a matter of luck. This
was really a fishing trip. He had cut several holes through
the surface ice and left baited hooks on lines. He had just
returned to the first hole he'd sawed when he spotted the
seal's nose poking out and got a shot in before the animal
noticed him. Normally to get a seal you have to find a hole
that you think one is using as a breathing hole and wait. You
have to stand really still with your harpoon ready. Seals can

stay underwater for twenty minutes, often longer – and they are easily spooked. He shrugs. And what about fish? 'Any bites yet?' you ask. 'One small capelin.' He nods towards the stowage rack on the back of the snowmobile. 'It's too soon to hope for more.' He's more lines to check later on.

The fishing lines Kuraluk has set up are in the same direction in which you are travelling. Tonight he will camp with you.

Seals: just what do you know about them? A Sealy Quiz.

1. Only one of these answers is **false**. Which is it?
   walruses use their tusks for:
   A. Fighting with each other.
   B. Hanging on to ice shelves when they want a rest.
   C. For levering the clams and mussels that they eat from the surfaces of the undersea rocks on which the shellfish live.

WALRUS

2. The Latin name for the walrus is *rosemarus*, which means rose of the sea, because sometimes their skin goes pink in colour. This colouring is because:

A. Walruses sunburn easily.

B. They get very hot while swimming and look red and flushed until they cool off – much like humans after exercise.

C. After fights between rival males, the loser often blushes with embarrassment.

3. You might come across a hooded seal with what looks like a big red bubble in front of its face. This is:

A. The seal blowing up the inner skin of its nostrils.

B. The seal eating its favourite meal – the lungs of another seal.

C. A seal spitting out some litter that's become trapped in its mouth.

MALE HOODED SEAL

4. True or false? All seals must give birth on land.

5. True or false? True seals (not including sea lions) rely mainly on blubber (fat) under their skin to keep warm.

6. True or false? Seals have no fur.

7. Which of these three statements is **false**? Eating bearded seals can be dangerous for people because:
A. Like Polar bears, their livers contain poisonous levels of Vitamin A.
B. Their flesh is acidic and burns your throat.
C. Their flesh often contain the eggs of tiny parasitic worms which can hatch inside the human body, making you ill.

BEARDED SEAL

8. Which of these answers is **false**? Baby seals do not go in the water because:
A. Their fluffy fur would be no good as insulation if it got soaked.
B. They have very little blubber.
C. They are unable to swim.

SEAL PUP

9. How do seals move about on land or ice?
A. Using their front flippers only.
B. Using their front and rear flippers.
C. By just wriggling their bodies.

10. True or False? Seals can only use breathing holes in the ice that are already there; they cannot cut new ones.

Answers on pages 56-57

Balloonists Killed by Worms!

On 11th July 1897 Swedish balloonist Salomon August Andrée set out for the North Pole with two companions, Nils Strinberg and Knut Fraenkel. Apart from a message which arrived several days later by carrier pigeon saying that things were fine, nothing more was heard of the explorers – not until 1930 when some seal hunters exploring a normally ice-bound island close to Franz Josef Land found their bodies, a canvas boat tied to a sledge and their equipment, including diaries.

This is Andrée's story ...

The expedition was beset with problems from the start. The balloon was enveloped in a freezing fog and forced lower and lower until it hit the ice and became wedged there. After thirteen hours, the men freed the balloon and carried on a short way, but the balloon

kept scraping the surface. The decision was made to continue to the pole on foot. The men dragged sledges for a month, but negotiating the cracked ice, the going was slow. Faced by worsening weather, the men decided that they would have to build a hut, shoot some animals for food and sit out the winter.

By mid-September things were getting worrying. Food supplies – ivory gulls and seals – were building up but the scent of the dead meat had attracted the attention

of polar bears. Worse, the pack ice, which the group was camped on, was starting to crack.

The ice split totally on October 1st (Andrée's diary said it was a perfect day, with guillemots and seals swimming close by when it happened). The camp was broken in two and the explorers found themselves floating away on a twenty-four-metre circle of ice, leaving behind two recently shot polar bears whose meat Andrée had thought would see them through the winter.

When sealers found the bodies of Andrée and his companions, it was clear from the large amount of food with them that the men had not died from hunger; nor, judging from their good equipment, from the cold. It looks like trichinosis contracted from eating poorly cooked seal meat killed them. They had been killed by worms!

ANSWERS from pages 50-52

1. **C.** It is now thought that walruses use their mouths not their tusks for prising shellfish off the seabed and rocks. Their moustaches of bristly whiskers help them feel around as they 'hoover' up their food.

2. **B.** As with humans, when walruses are hot, blood vessels close to the skin open up to allow more blood in, which is cooled by sea water or the air outside. That blood just under the skin makes it look pink. Incidentally, the name 'walrus' comes from the Norwegian *Val Russ* which means 'sea elephant'.

3. **A.** This is quite a gross trick to do - blow out the skin lining of your nostrils. Both males and females can do it, though males can blow bigger bubbles (males also have an inflatable blackish-grey skin sac on top of their heads). No one really knows why hooded seals do this. It could be aggressive males showing off or trying to attract females. Even lone, 'quiet' seals in zoos have been observed in this strange habit.

4. **TRUE.** Unlike whales and dolphins, which give birth in the water, baby seals are always born on land (or ice). They would drown and or die of cold otherwise.

5. **TRUE.** Except when they are newly born, when they have fur but have not yet developed blubber.

6. **FALSE.** They do have some but (except for baby seals) this has little use as insulation.

7. **B.** The livers of many arctic seals, especially older ones, contain poisonous levels of Vitamin A, the same vitamin found in carrots that improves our night vision. As with many other carnivores, bearded seals pick up worms in their shellfish and fish diet. These worms are passed on to animals eating them and can give them a disease called trichinosis (as our poor balloonist discovered).

8. **C.** They can swim though they have to learn how to hunt. Seals are born with little blubber to keep them warm. This they build up very rapidly through suckling their mothers' fat-rich milk. In the meantime they have a coat of fluffy fur to keep them warm. This makes baby seals prize commodities for the Inuit, who use the fur to line their boots among other things, and also for commercial hunters who kill thousands of harp seal pups for their skins each year. Unable to swim and without the protection of their mothers for long periods, baby seals are also prime targets for predatory polar bears and Arctic foxes.

9. **C.** Unlike sea lions, which can rise up on their flippers, true seals are far less mobile on land as they can only move around there by wriggling their bodies.

10. **FALSE.** Ringed seals have been known to use the short claws on their flippers to cut or saw through thin ice. Once they have opened up a breathing hole, they have to break off new ice that forms, threatening to cover it up.

The place that Kuraluk suggests for tonight's campsite appears much like anywhere else on the pack ice. But here, the seal hunter announces, producing a saw from the snowmobile's stowage rack, has just the right snow needed to build an igloo.

How to build an Igloo

The Inuit never live permanently in Igloos. They're more of a temporary shelter, used while travelling across snowy areas. Though their use has decreased in modern times, there are many still built in the traditional way.

- Mark out a circle about three metres in diameter.
- Using the saw, cut rectangular snow blocks each roughly 50 cm square.

It makes sense to cut your bricks from the floor of your igloo so that you end up with a flat raised area on one side for a sleeping
platform. If you want windows to let light in you can cut some bricks out of clear ice instead of snow.

- Lay the bricks round your circle slicing, each along the edges so that the walls tilt in slightly.
- Add a second layer (another way to build up is to work up in a spiral rather than one layer at a time).
- And a third (at this stage it is much easier, if working in pairs, for one person to stay inside).
- Finally you should end up with just a hole in the top. Cut a piece of snow to fit it. This is a key piece for the strength of the whole igloo and should be cut to exactly the right shape (by now one of you will be walled up inside).
- Use the saw to cut a doorway.
- Use handfuls of snow to stop up the gaps between your bricks.
- (Optional) Build an entrance passage to keep out the wind.

Your finished igloo!

Kuraluk sets up a *kudluk*, a seal-fat-heating fire - a raised metal pan with a blob of pinkish-white blubber. It gives off a surprising amount of light and heat, though not enough to melt the walls of the igloo. Forget those stories you've heard of Inuits wearing very little in their cosy snow homes. They obviously don't feel the cold as much as you. There may not be the wind chill in your shelter and it's warmer than outside, but it's hovering around zero degrees all the same.

'For you,' Kuraluk says, pointing to the sleeping platform. He's in the tent with Jimmy tonight.

Later ...

You sleep fitfully. You are aware of the wind building up outside - 'a real hooli' as Jimmy would say. Some snow flurries even blow through the entrance tunnel causing your kudluk flame to waver. You hear some muffled noise - the dogs complaining? One of your companions checking the loads on the sledges? Something scuffling against the wall of the igloo ...

You slip out of your sleeping bag, pull on your boots and take a peek outside.

The wind-blown snow and ice crystals sting your face and in the whiteout it's just possible to see a few metres in front of your face.

White on white. Something large. Lumbering. You make out the black tip of a nose, eyes...

Polar Bear!

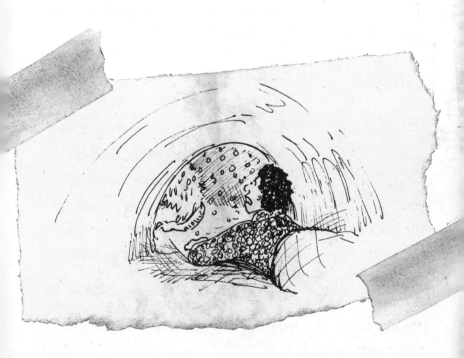

Chapter 5
POLAR BEAR

There's a huge, white bear outside your igloo. What should you do now?

Here are some choices. Choose now.

A. Stay absolutely still.

B. Slide back into the igloo.

C. Get out - to warn your friends or get the gun.

D. Shout, wave your arms and try to scare it off.

Look at this plan view of your camp. Think what the polar bear has come here for. Is it after you? Would any of the choices above change that situation?

Answer on page 66

A shot rings out. Then another. The bear starts and, with a surprising turn of speed, ambles off. You see Kuraluk pointing his rifle into the blizzard. Did he hit it. No, they were just warning shots. This bear knew to move when it heard them. Did you not notice the blue spray paint on its coat? Kuraluk asks. This one's obviously been marked. Maybe it's been raiding the refuse tip at the edge of Ninnuvulik. Persistent offenders have in the past been drugged and trucked – or helicoptered – far away from settlements (they still often return, so good is the navigational sense of polar bears).

Jimmy calms the dogs, which have become agitated, while Kuraluk checks the dead seal which he had covered over with snow before turning in for the night. The bear didn't get to it but it was a close thing. He should've known better than to leave the carcass so close to camp. The trouble is, now there's a polar bear hanging around,

it's probably better to get an early start rather than waiting for the bear to return. Jimmy starts dismantling the tent and re-stowing the loads on the sledges. Kuraluk will leave you now. He will check his fishing lines and then return to Ninnuvulik.

KURALUK

Some things you should know about polar bears ...

The largest land predators on Earth, polar bears are supremely adapted to their arctic environment. They spend their lives wandering vast distances across the coast and ice floes in search of seals, which form the main part of their diet. To do this they must have to have good senses to find their prey and the ability to catch it. They have to survive the polar cold and be able to swim between masses of floating ice. Polar bears have been found on ice over 200 kilometres from the nearest land. They can submerge for over a minute.

Surprisingly in this freezing climate, they have to be able to keep cool. All the exertion of chasing around, swimming and climbing in and out of the water can really heat you up.

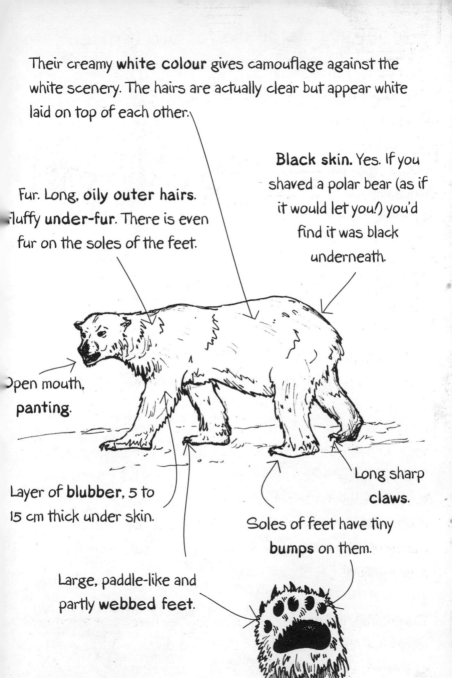

Their creamy **white colour** gives camouflage against the white scenery. The hairs are actually clear but appear white laid on top of each other.

Black skin. Yes. If you shaved a polar bear (as if it would let you!) you'd find it was black underneath.

Fur. Long, **oily outer hairs**. Fluffy **under-fur**. There is even fur on the soles of the feet.

Open mouth, **panting**.

Layer of **blubber**, 5 to 15 cm thick under skin.

Long sharp **claws**.

Soles of feet have tiny **bumps** on them.

Large, paddle-like and partly **webbed feet**.

Now, can you match the feature (written in the bold writing) with the reason for it?

1. Keeping warm _____ and _____
2. Absorbing heat _____
3. Gripping slippery ice _____ and _____
4. Cooling down _____
5. Keeping dry _____
6. Camouflage _____

Answers on page 68

ANSWER from page 62

A. This might work provided that the bear doesn't turn towards you – then it might decide you would make a better meal than the dead seal it has sniffed out.

B. Probably the best option. BUT: You won't know what's going on outside – or if the polar bear has decided to investigate you further ... you could always kick out the wall and escape out the back, but is that wise?

C. Only worth risking if you are sure the polar bear has moved on, otherwise you probably would draw its attention.

D. Are you mad? In this wind it probably won't hear you, but if you did want the full attention of more than half a tonne of the world's largest land carnivore, I'm sure you could get it.

So, if you're the biggest, toughest land predator on the planet, is there anything at all you need to worry about? Killer whales attacking while you are swimming (rare, but it does happen), angry walruses (again, unusual but possible) ... other polar bears ... and sadly, most of all, **people** hunting you.

POLAR BEAR
SWIMMING

The other thing that can be a killer is the weather, in particular the freezing cold of that long winter. It is dark, blizzarding, and there's virtually no food around. This is a good time to seal yourself up in a burrow and sit out the worst of the weather and, if you are an expectant mother polar bear, give birth and nurse your young. Adults don't eat during this time. They just live off the fat reserves they put on in the summer, often for months.

Starvation is a major problem. To keep a large carnivore like a polar bear going you need a lot of fuel. Your main prey – ringed and bearded seals – is spread out over vast areas and

1. Under-fur and blubber.
2. Black skin.
3. Claws (also good for gripping slippery seals) and bumps.
4. Panting (heat is also conducted away from the shoulders, nose and ears).
5. Oily outer hairs.
6. White colour.

is hard to find, let alone sneak up and catch. Your life is one of a solitary wanderer constantly on the hunt for food. You have to walk and swim great distances because if you don't, then you don't eat, then you die. Life is hard as a top predator.

Soon the sledges are loaded and you are on your way again. The wind has dropped but a mist of fine snow swirls around hampering visibility in the dim morning light. The feel of the ice surface through the sledge is somehow different. In some places the runners glide effortlessly over the fresh, crisp snow. Elsewhere, the lumpy ice underneath causes the sledge to lurch unpredictably. You bump past ridges and mounds of compacted ice. You can hear a deep groaning rumbling creaking as if the whole ice sheet is flexing. The dogs, seeming to sense the change, slacken their pace. One ridge is littered with gigantic ice blocks. You and Jimmy have to manoeuvre the teams and sledges around the obstacles, using your ice-axes in places to hack a clear path through the fractured ice. Then for a while you are on to flat frozen sea ice again and your sledges are careering along. Suddenly you hear Jimmy screaming 'Whoa!'. You know what to do. Throw out the snow hooks. Stop the sledge. You secure the sledge and walk over to Jimmy.

The way ahead is blocked by a 'lead' of open water. The crack in the ice is not large – about the length of the sledge – but it is too wide to cross. You will have to detour, but before you do, you decide to check your location. You extract the GPS from your pack and wait while it computes your position.

The coordinates it gives you are totally confusing. You can't be in that place!

1. If you are to believe what the screen says then you have ended up south of your igloo camp, even though you've been travelling north, and ...
2. If you are to believe your compass, you've not been travelling north at all, but east.

Just what is going on? Read on to find out ...

Chapter 6
GOING WITH THE FLOE

You have travelled north but now you are further south. The 'north' direction on your GPS is east according to your compass.

Can you solve these riddles?

Decide whether these suggestions are possible solutions.

1. Your GPS is malfunctioning.
2. Your GPS 'compass' pointer is pointing to true north, not magnetic north which is to the west of you.
3. You have travelled over the North Pole without realising it and so now you are travelling south without even changing direction.
4. The Earth's magnetic north pole has changed position.
5. The ice that you are on is floating southwards.

All could have happened . . .

1. Possible, though unlikely that you would get a clear reading if it were.
2. The Earth's magnetic North pole is at present over the sea above northern Canada. The magnetic North pole is the place on the surface where the Earth's magnetic field lines come together. This is

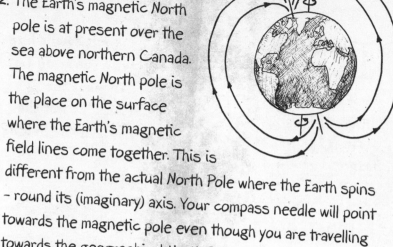

different from the actual North Pole where the Earth spins – round its (imaginary) axis. Your compass needle will point towards the magnetic pole even though you are travelling towards the geographical North Pole.
3. Possible. Remember, at the North Pole the only direction would be south. You can travel in a straight line right over it, northwards

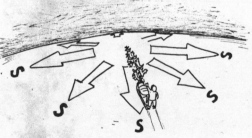

then southwards without changing direction.
4. Possible, if you were close to the magnetic pole. Its position moves around 15 kilometres each year. After shifting southwards during previous centuries it is now moving to the North. In one day, the position of the pole ovals round roughly 80 kilometres from its average centre point.
5. A real problem for polar explorers – now it seems the first man credited with getting to the North Pole didn't actually get there ...

Peary and the Pole

The problem with getting to the North Pole is how do you know when you've arrived? You're on flat, featureless ice pack and it's not exactly as if the geographical top of the world is marked. It's not the same as the magnetic north pole either. All the Earth's magnetic-field lines converge somewhere in the sea above northern Canada and that position moves greatly over the years (even in a day). A compass will be no help in finding the geographic North Pole. Before the invention of satellite global-positioning systems, explorers had to find their location by measuring accurately the angle above the horizon of the sun or the stars.

ROBERT PEARY

Admiral Robert Peary of the US Navy was desperate to be the first man to reach the North Pole. It was his life's ambition and he was determined nothing would stop him being the first to get there. Around the turn of the twentieth century, he led four expeditions with that aim. On the third trip, in 1905, he lost all but his little toes (see Chapter 1), but he decided to have one last go in 1909. By now he was 54 and he knew this would be his last attempt. He organised teams of sailors and Inuit to travel before him, setting up supply dumps and building igloos, which he would use for his final push to the Pole. By all accounts, Peary, determined (or desperate) to get to the Pole first was not a nice man to work with, especially if you were one of his Inuit servants. He

PEARY AND HENSON

finally got there along with his black American assistant, Matt Henson, and four Inuit (Ooqueah, Ootah, Egingwah and Seegloo) on 7th April 1909. When they returned, Peary expected all the glory for himself, but it turned out someone else claimed to have reached the Pole first.

As an assistant on one of his previous polar expeditions, Frederick Cook had grown to hate the admiral. Now he said he had arrived at the Pole a full year before Peary. Peary said Cook was lying. The feud was huge news in all the newspapers at the time. When it was showed

FREDERICK COOK

that Cook had faked a photo of himself supposedly climbing Mount McKinley in Alaska, the National Geographical Society studied his polar log books and decided he couldn't possibly have crossed the ice to the Pole in the time that he said. Peary was declared the winner of the race to the North Pole. (This incidentally made the great Norwegian explorer, Roald Amundsen change his North Pole plans to South Pole ones; he got there first, just pipping Britain's Captain Scott to the post in 1912.)

But! No one checked Peary's polar log in detail until a little later, and mighty dodgy it looked too. No doubt he had come close to the Pole but had he actually got there? It now seems doubtful. Knowing this would be his last trip, in his desperation to get there first, it seems he might have rigged his navigational calculations.

And the first person to reach the North Pole? Well, Amundsen was one of the first to see it. He flew over in an airship with Nobile, among others, in 1925, making him the first person to see both Poles. But he did not land there. In was not until 1968 that the first people arrived there overland (well, over the ice). That was by snowmobile. A year later a British expedition led by Wally Herbert succeeded in crossing the Arctic ice via the Pole with husky-pulled sledges. In 1974, the Japanese explorer, Naomi Uemura, also got there under dog power. He did it single-handedly.

Back to your situation ...

A lead in the ice crosses your route. You are drifting southwards as you travel north. North on your compass is towards the real west.

There are decisions to make. Decide what you will do ...

1. Look at this map of your route so far and your compass. Which two of the options 1-5 listed at the start of this chapter are most likely?

2. What should you and Jimmy do now?
   A. Carry on straight ahead. You might just make it.
   B. Travel east to see if you can find the end of the lead
   C. Travel west to see if you can find the end of the lead
   D. Stop to assess your situation. Is the lead opening or closing?

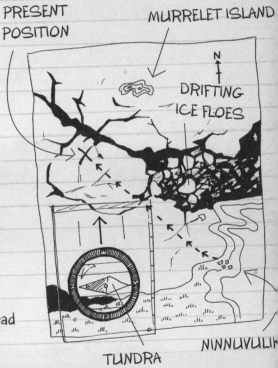

PRESENT POSITION

MURRELET ISLAND

DRIFTING ICE FLOES

N

TUNDRA

NINNUVULIK

As night approaches, you see the gap is closing as ice is forming across it. Does this change the situation? Should you wait for it to freeze fully over, then cross with the dogs and sledge?

Answers on page 77

If anything the lead appears to be opening, but it's hard to tell. After a couple of hours of waiting, Jimmy makes the decision that you should loop round to the west. You drive your two teams of dogs on slowly now, constantly aware of the ice groaning and creaking beneath you. At one point it starts to crack. You see seawater welling up around the sledge's runners and you urge the dogs to speed up before the broken ice tips even more. It's a close thing. You can tell you're on floating ice and you do your best to get your team over this section, even though more than once it seems that the floe is breaking up all around you. You reach a shelf

of ice that sits above the main ice floe – maybe it was once part of an iceberg that broke off a glacier. This freshwater ice floats higher than the denser sea ice. Briefly you rest and check the GPS. The news is good. You've made progress or maybe it's just that the sea currents are taking the floating ice in the direction you want to go. You know you have to keep moving, however. Icebergs may have the bulk of their mass concentrated under the water line, but bits are breaking off constantly. Your 'safe' platform could tip or even topple right over at any time.

Finally you reach ice, which Jimmy says has long been frozen and perhaps safer to make camp on than the thin new ice you've taken such risks crossing. There's another reason he wants to make camp now. It's snowing. Visibility is dropping. Whiteout. It would be foolhardy to carry on.

ANSWERS from page 75

1. **2.** Magnetic north is to your actual west and **5.** You are on an ice floe that is moving south.
2. **D.** Before making a long detour, it is worth checking if the lead is opening, closing or even freezing over. If you can't tell, go back to the last pressure ridge where you might get more of a view. With luck you might be able to see if the lead narrows or closes in one direction. You may have a long journey or a long wait. It could mean a way across, but test the way first with your ski poles or the end of your ice-axe. And stay roped to Jimmy while you do this.

Chapter 7
HOOLI

'It looks like it's going to be a real **hooli**', Jimmy says grimly shaking the snow off his parka as he pulls himself into the tent. Despite the snow you've piled round its extended 'skirts', the wind seems intent on lifting it into the air. The dome shape has become more a flattened 's' as the wind pounds the structure, bending the flexible aluminium poles.

There's nothing to do but sit it out.

The dogs will be fine, wrapped in their tails.

There's little point in you checking your team.

1. The wind could blow you over
2. You could get lost in the whiteout.
3. Even your 'windproof' coat can't stop your body heat being sapped by that degree of 'wind chill'.
4. If you fell over or remained where you were, you'd soon start your own personal snowdrift.

But what is snow? Why is it so different from ice? And what is this sea ice you've been nearly crashing through for most of the last chapter. It's time you knew the facts.

Ice and Snow: the Facts

Pure water freezes into ice at 0 degrees centigrade. Seawater contains dissolved salt and that doesn't freeze until the temperature is below zero – on average 1.8 degrees centigrade, lower if the water is saltier. So would the pack ice you're camped on (the surface of the sea that has frozen) taste salty?

The answer is: it depends how old it is. Newly formed sea ice is salty but over time, the dissolved salt is pulled downwards by gravity. Seawater ice that's been frozen a year or so would taste no different to you than ice from fresh water. Also as old sea ice contains less salt to weigh it down it would float slightly higher than the newly formed stuff ... which brings us on to ...

Icebergs. These towering lumps of ice are made from freshwater ice that has fallen off glaciers (rivers of ice) that flow into the sea (Most arctic icebergs have fallen off the glaciers round Greenland). When water freezes it expands (gets bigger). As it is more spread out than liquid water, it's less dense – lighter compared to the same amount of water – so it floats. But, it's true what they say about the 'tip of the iceberg': most of its bulk is actually under the water, on average 80 to 90 per cent of it. As icebergs get pushed around by ocean currents, they smash into each other and into pack ice and bits melt. Never take a boat close to an iceberg: you might hit the submerged bit you can't see or part of the top might fall on you. In the worst case, the whole iceberg might topple over and you'd be pulled under by the enormous current produced.

Not all icebergs are white. Depending on impurities in the ice as the berg formed, or sometimes because of the way the sun lights them, some icebergs have a definite blue or green tint.

Snow. This is formed from water vapour freezing in clouds. Snowflakes often form when water molecules clump around dust particles. Because of the way water molecules are shaped and the forces that hold together the atoms of hydrogen and oxygen in the H_2O molecule, snowflakes usually form as regular six-sided crystals. No two are exactly alike. Generally speaking, spikier, thinner crystals are formed quicker at colder temperatures. The crystals are clear but the effect of millions on top of each other, scattering the light, makes them appear white (in the same way that clear polar-bear hairs look white – see Chapter 5).

So is all that dusting of fine powder swirling around your tent made up of trillions of perfectly formed crystals? Highly unlikely. In the daytime much of the snow near the surface melts and goes slushy (yes, even in the high Arctic). At night it freezes again. Most of the ground covering you'd call 'snow-ice', is a re-frozen mixture of snow and ice crystals. It's the light top layer that's constantly being picked up by the wind and blasting raw those exposed patches of skin which your goggles and hood don't quite cover.

You and Jimmy are hunkered down in the shelter of your tent. You can tell snow is building up on its windward side, but at least the wind seems to have lessened. You don't feel the tent is in immediate danger of taking off any more.

Sitting the snowstorm out is boring. There's nothing to do except make notes in your diary and play cards with Jimmy and those activities soon lose their appeal. You can't even cook up any food to eat. Even if you braved the weather conditions to retrieve the cooking gear from its bag stowed on your sledge, Jimmy will not let you set up your stove inside the tent. It would be unsafe, he says. You could easily set fire to all your equipment – and your only shelter (this has happened on trips before) and then where would you be? Jimmy zips himself up in his sleeping bag and says he's going to sleep out the hooli.

So you sit … and wait … and get bored.

The wind appears to have dropped. You unzip the tent inner, then the flysheet, and knock away the small drift of snow that's covering the entrance. The wind is still gusting, blasting you with ice crystals as you pull yourself out, but the snow has stopped. You can see a faint disc of sunlight through the low cloud cover.

Your dogs lift their muzzles from under their ice-encrusted tails. As you throw them the chunks of seal meat for which they've been so patiently waiting, your eyes catch on the only feature in this white-on-white scenery. It looks like a low rocky cliff though the blowing ice blurs its outline. Murrelet Island? Your GPS puts you under a kilometre away from its position. You're there! You sat through that storm never realising how close you were to your final destination. Now you could be minutes from finding out the truth about Nobile's airship. You could be on the verge of making your discovery.

No time to lose. You grab your **'day pack'** with your **sleeping bag**, **bivvy bag**, **snow shovel**, **flare pistol** and **spare food**, strap on your skis . . . and off you go. As you push off with your poles and start the back-forward scissoring of your legs to get yourself going on your cross-country **skis**, a sense of foreboding slips through your thoughts. Isn't there something you've forgotten to do?

The ice pack here is smooth and, with the fresh dusting of snow, it's a relatively quick and easy journey to Murrelet Island though. Soon you're sweating with the exertion of repeatedly sliding the skis forwards then pushing back. You make towards some lines you can see standing out against the white. They're hard to make out through the blowing snow flurries but they look like gigantic ribs – the internal structure of an airship! This must surely be Nobile's lost craft, *Italia*. You now need some evidence to show your theory about its location was right. Ignoring the flakes of falling snow that are starting to swirl around you, you press on forwards.

That feeling of doubt is still gnawing at you.
1. What have you forgotten to do?
2. What will you notice when you turn to head back?
3. What piece of kit for finding your way have you not brought with you?

Answers on page 86

The metal struts are twisted, buckled and encrusted with ice. There are still some fragments of the fabric that once covered the dirigible's frame. You can make out some letters on one of the pieces – 'ALIA'. Nearby there is an iced-over pile of stones. Surely someone put that there. You pull the stones aside, revealing a wooden box – maybe it was once a case for delicate instruments but now, after years of freezing and thawing, it crumbles as you lift it. The notebook inside is still intact, though, and you realise this could be the logbook that reveals what happened to the remainder of Nobile's crew, who floated off with the airship after its first crash on to the ice. Just wait until Jimmy hears the news!

You turn round to face your camp and, with a stab of stark terror, you realise what you have forgotten to do.

ANSWERS from page 84

1. You didn't tell Jimmy that you were setting off.
2. The snow is swirling round so much you can no longer see your camp.
3. You've not brought your GPS, which might have given you a heading to where your camp is (remember your compass is all but useless this close to the Magnetic north pole).

How stupid you were for setting off alone! Your life is now in serious danger. Will you do the right things now to survive? Find out in the next chapter ...

Chapter 8
SURVIVE OR DIE!

Zero visibility, sub-zero temperatures, and an evil wind chill.
Can you survive the blizzard?

Start off with **50 life points**. Each time you make a wrong
decision, you lose points as the effect of the cold -
hypothermia - starts to kick in. If your points get to zero,
you lose consciousness. Will you survive?

1. These are your options. Choose which one you will do.
   a. Stay where you are. Go to 3.
   b. Carry on forwards to the shelter of the rocks that
      you saw. Go to 6.
   c. Get back to your camp. Go to 9.

2. A bad choice if you decide to move. You'll lose heat for
   one thing and you'll most likely become more lost. Go to
   6. If you decided to stay put, go to 11.

3. The wind is howling around you. You can feel your body heat leaking away. You will need to quickly improvise some sort of shelter – and the only building material you have is snow. What piece of kit should you get out to build a windbreak? Go to 7.

4. You could fire a flare, though in this blizzard it's highly unlikely that Jimmy will see it (-10 points if you didn't get this right). It feels like you've been here for ages. Should you stay here or move your position? Go to 2.

5. The early stages of hypothermia could be affecting you (-10 points if you didn't get this right). What could you do for extra energy? Go to 8.

6. Not a good choice. The chances are you'll just get yourself even more lost … and colder (-40 points). Reconsider your options. Go back to 1.

7. Use your shovel. In these conditions, building an igloo would be too difficult but you could quickly dig a hollow to shelter from the wind. If 'shovel' wasn't the answer you thought of, subtract 10 points. What two pieces of kit should you use now to keep warm? Go to 10.

8. Eat your chocolate (-10 points if you didn't get this right). What could you use to signal Jimmy? Go to 4.

9. Not a good choice. Your GPS might have been helpful here (if you'd remembered to bring it and had stored the position of your camp in its memory). You're going to become colder and more disorientated. After floundering around in the whiteout for a few minutes, you soon realise you have to reconsider your options (-30 points). Go back to 1.

10. Sleeping bag and bivvy bag. Get into them now (-10 points for each one you didn't get right). You're finding it difficult to think straight. What could be wrong with you? Go to 5.

11. The right thing to do. Not guaranteed for your survival, but you've done all the right things to maximise your chances.

So, what happens next?

If you dropped to zero points, you lost consciousness. In all likelihood Jimmy would not have found you until you had become frostbitten, or died. You might have been smothered by snow and never found.

If you survived…

The next few hours are tough. You are reasonably snug in your bivvy bag and sleeping bag in your hollow in the snow, though parts of your face, which are exposed, may succumb to frost nip. Drifting snow partially covers you. You fight to remain awake. You know that if sleep takes hold then you're dead.

Suddenly, you are aware of Jimmy's face in front of yours. You can hear his voice shouting above the wind, 'Are you all right? Are you all right?' With his help you pull yourself out of your bivvy bag and clip on your skis.

Clear-headed now, you know exposure hasn't set in, but you need to get out of this chilling wind and get into the shelter of your tent. You try to apologise to Jimmy for being so stupid as to go off alone, but he just shrugs and clips you on to the end of the rope he has tied round his waist. He gives you a moment to gather up your stuff and put on your skis, checks the direction back to the camp on his GPS, then he sets off.

Mercifully soon, you reach the welcoming sight of your campsite – your dome tent, the two sledges and lines of dogs – in a surprisingly short amount of time. You were only three or four hundred metres away when you became lost …

The Fate of the Airship *Italia*

May 25th 1928: Italian aviator Umberto Nobile's airship, *Italia*, fell out of the sky and crashed on to the Arctic pack ice. This had been Nobile's second trip by airship across the North Pole. The other had been with the great Polar explorer Roald Amundsen two years previously.

This time Nobile and his crew of fourteen Italians and a Swede had over flown the pole successfully when they hit a bank of freezing fog. With ice forming over its cloth 'envelope', the airship started losing height at an alarming rate. Even tilting the nose of the craft upwards, its three propeller engines going at full throttle could do little to slow the descent.

When she hit, one man died and nine others along with what turned out to be some vital equipment – tent, radio, food, red dye – were pitched out on to the ice. Then, its load lightened, *Italia*,

with six men still aboard, blew away in the ferocious
wind, never to be seen again.

Two of the survivors (including Nobile, who had
broken an arm and a leg) were injured. The others
were fine. They dyed their tent red to make it
conspicuous to rescuers and tried to radio for help.
Their 'Mayday' messages never got through, though
they did receive broadcasts saying that a search was
under way. Amundsen himself got involved but lost his
life when his plane crashed somewhere among the
drifting ice floes.

Meanwhile, the ice floe that Nobile's group were camped on drifted south in sight of an island. Three of the men decided to head out across the ice for it, but the section they were on broke off and started floating northwards. Each day they trekked towards the island, then found they were further away than before. Two of the men survived and were eventually picked up by a Russian icebreaker.

The six remaining Italians waiting in the red tent became depressed each time their ice floe floated out of sight of the island. They kept sending distress calls but could hear that the ships and planes searching for them were in totally the wrong area. Then their luck changed. A radio operator in Russia picked up one of their SOS calls and soon a seaplane was directed to fly low over the ice and drop supplies. Another plane landed on the ice and picked up Nobile. When it returned to fetch the others, it crashed; the pilot and the four stranded airship men had to wait until the Russian icebreaker finally made it through.

And the hero of the story? Was it Nobile who led his men and kept their morale up as they waited for weeks in the small red tent on the drifting ice floe? Was it Amundsen who lost his life searching for his former compatriot?

Maybe that honour should go to Nobile's pet dog, Titina. She saw off a polar bear that ambled in to investigate the strange red tent. Picture the scene. It certainly had the downed airship men in fits of laughter at the time – a knee-high pooch yapping at the heels of the world's largest land predator, driving it across the ice until finally it dived into the freezing sea to escape its tormentor.

Jimmy warms you up with some hot chocolate from his Thermos flask and you start to regain some of your heat as you're back in the cosy tent. Now you are safe you can look at the notebook you found by the airship's ribs. It's thawing out and is slightly soggy. Separating the pages is difficult. Rather than being the logbook you had hoped for, it's full of navigational tables. But there is some writing on the first page - some coordinates - and a crudely drawn map. Below, there are three signatures: Luigi Lopiccolo, Guiseppi... something - you can't make out the rest. The third signature is indecipherable. The three who signed their names were obviously the last survivors of the Airship *Italia* and this map showed the route they set out on, on their final march to what they must have hoped would be salvation. You know they never made it. Their fate remains a mystery.

What will you do now? It's too late in the year to continue the expedition to find out what happened to those three men as, with summer approaching, the ice floes will be breaking up. No. Go back and announce your discovery of the lost Airship Italia. An achievement like that will be an international sensation. The spotlight of the world's press will be on you. There'll be TV interviews to do, and reports to write for the Geographical Society.

Don't forget to mention the help you've had along the way. You couldn't have got this far without Jimmy Asecaq and the huskies that pulled your sledge. What about the hunter, Kuraluk, and the excellent igloo that he built?

But how will you get back? That could be as treacherous as the journey here. Look at the map on the next page and decide which hexagons you travelled through on your journey to Murrelet Island. Here are some hints:

· You flew across the tundra to Ninnuvulik ...
· Then set out across the ice and met Kuraluk, who built you an igloo where you were bothered by a polar bear ...
· You crossed the breaking ice floes across a 'lead' of open water ...
· Then pushed on through worsening weather to your destination.

Answer on page 100

You've proved yourself a skilled explorer of the Arctic ice cap, so what next? More snow and ice? Try climbing the high HIMALAYAS. Or would you like to branch out to warmer climes? Maybe the SAHARA DESERT or the SOUTH SEA ISLANDS are more to your taste?

Explorers Wanted!

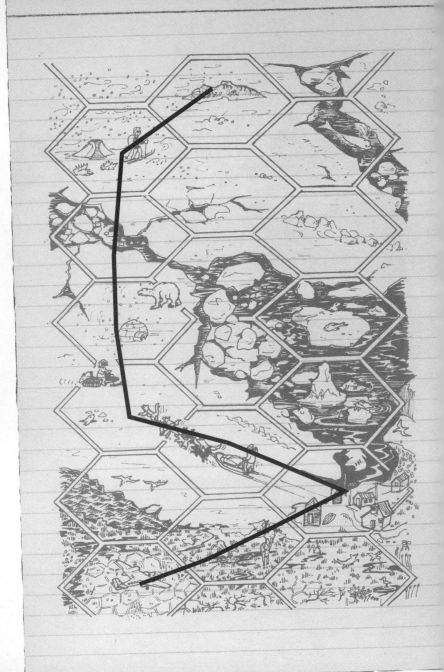

Your mission ... should you choose to accept it, is to journey through the blazing Sahara desert in search of a lost canyon, lake and waterfall. Will you take up the challenge?

If anyone can help you survive out there, Chapman can ... Read the mission notes from a real live **Indiana Jones.**

'Egmont's wonderful Explorers Wanted! series by Simon Chapman perfectly illustrates that dumbing-down is not necessary to make utterly readable narrative non-fiction'
Guardian

'Crystal clear information, with an adventure along the way. Simon Chapman is a real explorer – and a great writer too'
Child Literacy

SIMON CHAPMAN'S
EXPLORERS
WANTED!
IN THE DESERT

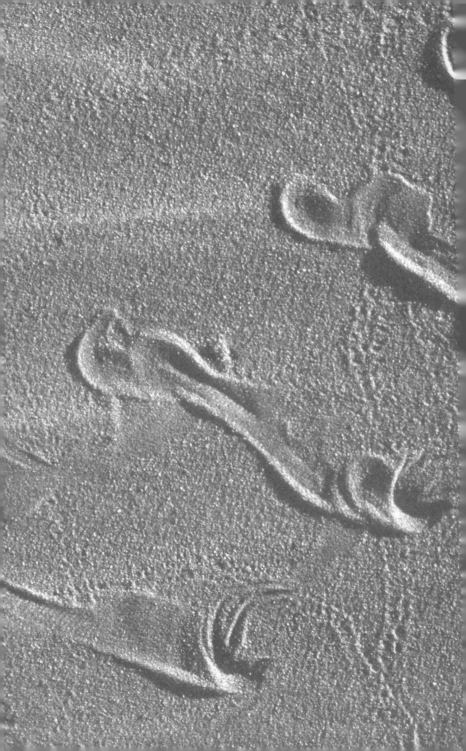

SO...YOU WANT TO EXPLORE THE SAHARA DESERT?

You want to...

... Traverse the endless **dunes** by camel...?

...Drink your fill in a **sparkling oasis**...?

...Encounter the **exotic people** and **strange creatures** that inhabit this arid wasteland...?

If the answer to any of these questions is **YES**, then this is the book for you so **Read on**...

THIS BOOK GIVES YOU the essential lowdown on life in this land of extremes, from how to cope with the intense heat and burning sun to **where you might find water** where at first glance there appears to be none. There'll also be the stories of some of the people who came before you, how they survived (or didn't!) in this, the greatest desert on Earth.

YOUR MISSION ... should you choose to accept it, is to get to the Ahaggan massif. Beyond the miles of flat gravel pans, the rocky *hammada* and the great sand sea of Najmer stands a huge slab of rock, sculpted over the centuries by wind-blown sand into fantastic pinnacles and deep gorges, which the sun's rays never reach. The Tuareg camel caravans of the deep desert have avoided the Ahaggan over the years. There was no water or forage for their animals. It was too easy to lose yourself in the treacherous terrain. Until recently that is ... Forced to shelter in the rocks by a sudden sandstorm, a group of nomads, separated from their caravan made a startling discovery. WATER. Cool and fresh and lots of it. When they finally made it out of the sand sea and *hammada* rock fields, the men told stories of a lost canyon with a lake and even a waterfall.

Painted on the canyon's walls were figures of giraffes, hippos and zebra, animals of the African plains not the Sahara desert. Seeing the state the men were in when they were found, few believed their story, especially as they could not explain how to get back to the valley.

So what is the truth? Could there really be a waterfall in the desert? What about the rock paintings? Who drew them and when? This is what you've set yourself to find out. Getting there will be some adventure. Just how will you start?

DJELLA OASIS

WELL AT BILAN

SAND SEA OF NAJMER

AHAGGAN MASSIF

Time to set the scene . . .

The Sahara desert is HUGE...

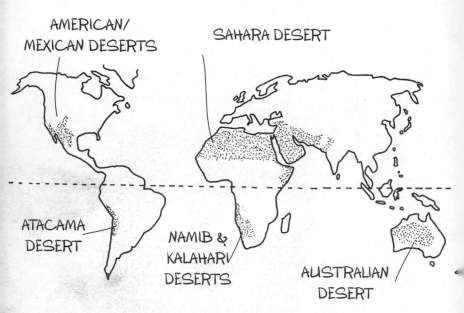

AMERICAN/
MEXICAN DESERTS

SAHARA DESERT

ATACAMA
DESERT

NAMIB &
KALAHARI
DESERTS

AUSTRALIAN
DESERT

It stretches right the way across the top of Africa and other deserts carry on beyond that through Arabia, the Middle East as far as southern Pakistan and western India. Here it is hot, dry and parched. The ground is rocky or sandy, in some places dotted with hardy plants that can endure the intense heat and lack of water, in other places totally barren. The Sahara and Middle East aren't the only hot deserts. If you look at a map of the world you'll notice other deserts, like the Namib and the Kalahari, mirrored across the equator in southern Africa. And if you look at North and South America

you'll notice the same thing, desert in both north and south,
jungle in between.

It's all to do with the way the sun heats the Earth. At the
equator, hot air rises (it's called convection). Moist air from
the oceans rushes in, so everything's wet and jungly. The air
- no moisture in it - falls at the Tropics of Cancer and

TROPIC OF
CANCER

EQUATOR

TROPIC OF
CAPRICORN

AIR FALLS

HOT AIR
RISES

AIR FALLS

Capricorn. Those areas are deserts. Generally the winds
blow away from there, taking away any moisture. So it's
mostly cloudless, hot and incredibly dry. But are all deserts
the same?

Certainly many desert animals across the
world have developed similar adaptations ...

SAHARA DESERT

FENNEC FOX

JERBOA

HORNED VIPER

MEXICAN DESERT

KANGAROO RAT

KIT FOX

SIDEWINDER
RATTLESNAKE

Take a look at this desert scene and the facts labelling it. Remember, this book is about the Sahara. Which four of the labels are wrong for North Africa?

DROMEDARY

CACTUS

JERBOA

1. Wild dromedary, one-humped camels.
2. Jerboa.
3. Nearly the entire desert is sandy.
4. It never rains.
5. Night-time can be very cold.
6. Cactus.

Mission notes

Mission notes

Mission notes

Mission notes

About the author

Writer and broadcaster, Simon Chapman, is a self-confessed jungle addict, making expeditions whenever he can. His travels have taken him to tropical forests all over the world, from Borneo and Irian Jaya to the Amazon.

The story of his search for a mythical Giant Ape in the Bolivian rainforest, *The Monster of the Madidi*, was published in 2001. He has also had numerous articles and illustrations published in magazines in Britain and the US, including *Wanderlust*, *BBC Wildlife* and *South American Explorer*, and has written and recorded for BBC Radio 4, and lectured on the organisation of jungle expeditions at the Royal Geographical Society, of which he is a fellow. When not exploring, Simon lives with his wife and his two young children in Lancaster, where he teaches physics in a high school.

EXPLORERS WANTED!

CALLING ALL EXPLORERS!

We hope that you've enjoyed this **EXPLORERS WANTED!** adventure.

To help us make our next books even more exciting, we'd love to hear from you. We want you to tell us what you liked best about this book, and which places you think **EXPLORERS WANTED!** should go in the future.

In return, we'll keep you informed about the series, author events that Simon Chapman might be involved in and, of course, fantastic competitions and give-aways.

The first 1,000 letters we receive will win a limited-edition **EXPLORERS WANTED!** badge to show off to their friends!

Send your ideas and comments to:

Simon Chapman
c/o Publicity Department
Egmont Books Limited
239 Kensington High Street
London
W8 6SA

More **EXPLORERS WANTED!**
titles for you to collect!

SIMON CHAPMAN'S
EXPLORERS
WANTED!
IN THE JUNGLE

SIMON CHAPMAN'S
EXPLORERS
WANTED!
IN THE HIMALAYAS

SIMON CHAPMAN'S
EXPLORERS
WANTED
ON SAFARI

SIMON CHAPMAN'S
EXPLORERS WANTED!
IN THE WILDERNESS

SIMON CHAPMAN'S
EXPLORERS WANTED!
ON THE SOUTH SEA ISLANDS

SIMON CHAPMAN'S
EXPLORERS WANTED!
AT THE NORTH POLE

SIMON CHAPMAN'S
EXPLORERS WANTED!
UNDER THE SEA